The War of 1812

Kevin Cunningham

AV² provides enriched content that supplements and complements this book. Weigl's AV² books strive to create inspired learning and engage young minds in a total learning experience.

Your AV² Media Enhanced books come alive with...

Audio
Listen to sections of the book read aloud.

Key Words
Study vocabulary, and complete a matching word activity.

Video
Watch informative video clips.

Quizzes
Test your knowledge.

Go to www.av2books.com, and enter this book's unique code.

BOOK CODE

AVZ73769

Embedded Weblinks
Gain additional information for research.

Slide Show
View images and captions, and prepare a presentation.

AV² by Weigl brings you media enhanced books that support active learning.

Try This!
Complete activities and hands-on experiments.

... and much, much more!

Published by AV² by Weigl
350 5th Avenue, 59th Floor
New York, NY 10118
Website: www.av2books.com

Library of Congress Cataloging-in-Publication Data
Names: Cunningham, Kevin, 1966- author.
Title: The War of 1812 / Kevin Cunningham.
Description: New York, NY : AV2 by Weigl, 2020. | Series: Building our nation | Audience: K to Grade 3.
Identifiers: LCCN 2018053480 (print) | LCCN 2018054382 (ebook) | ISBN 9781489698964 (Multi User ebook) | ISBN 9781489698971 (Single User ebook) | ISBN 9781489698940 (hardcover : alk. paper) | ISBN 9781489698957 (softcover : alk. paper)
Subjects: LCSH: United States--History--War of 1812--Juvenile literature.
Classification: LCC E354 (ebook) | LCC E354 .C87 2020 (print) | DDC 973.5/2--dc23
LC record available at https://lccn.loc.gov/2018053480

Printed in Guangzhou, China
1 2 3 4 5 6 7 8 9 0 23 22 21 20 19

012019
102318

Project Coordinator: John Willis   Designer: Ana María Vidal

Every reasonable effort has been made to trace ownership and to obtain permission to reprint copyright material. The publishers would be pleased to have any errors or omissions brought to their attention so that they may be corrected in subsequent printings.

Weigl acknowledges Alamy, Bridgeman Images, Getty Images, Shutterstock, and Wikimedia as its primary image suppliers for this title.

First published in 2019 by North Star Editions

CONTENTS

Many U.S. ships could not get past the British blockade.

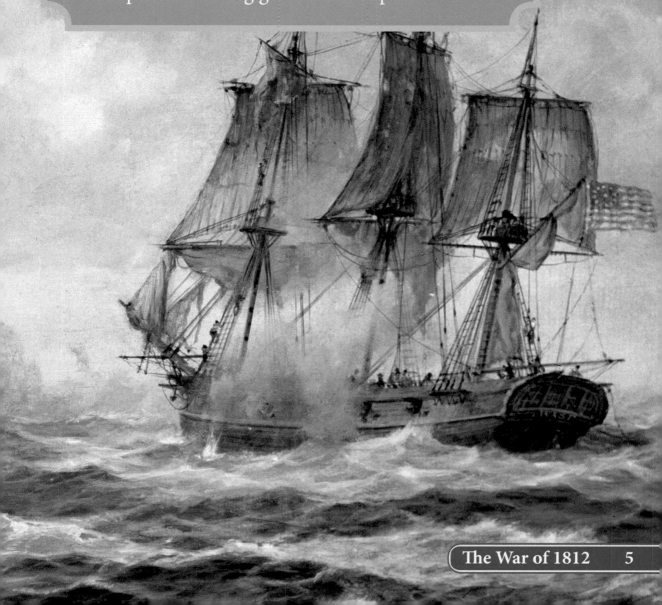

Chapter 1
Reasons for War

In the early 1800s, the French and the British were at war. The fighting took place in Europe. But it affected people in the United States. Starting in 1807, the British used their powerful navy to stop U.S. trade with France. They created a **blockade**. It kept U.S. ships from selling goods in Europe.

The British hoped to weaken France. But the blockade hurt the United States, too. Cities such as Baltimore and Boston relied on trade. They lost a lot of money. And because less trade was happening, the U.S. government collected less tax money. As a result, the United States had trouble paying its bills.

The British Royal Navy also used impressment. This meant that British captains forced people to serve as sailors on their ships. Some of these people were not even British. Between 1807 and 1812, the Royal Navy forced more than 6,000 U.S. citizens to work on its ships. This angered many people.

Some U.S. citizens were forced to serve on British ships after being mistaken for British citizens.

The United States also faced problems on the **frontier** near the Great Lakes. Settlers were spreading to this land. But Native Americans already lived there. They fought against the newcomers.

Many Native American groups, such as the Shawnees, became **allies** with the British. For this reason, many U.S. settlers blamed the British for tensions with Native Americans in this area. Sometimes settlers attacked the Native Americans. But this only convinced more groups to join the British.

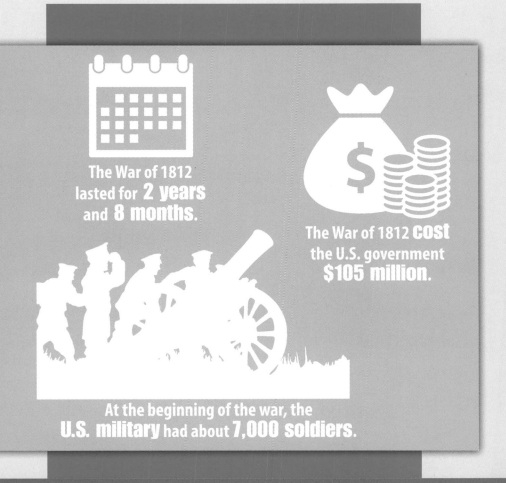

The War of 1812 lasted for **2 years** and **8 months**.

The War of 1812 **cost** the U.S. government **$105 million**.

At the beginning of the war, the **U.S. military** had about **7,000 soldiers**.

The United States and the British tried to **negotiate**. But U.S. settlers kept taking native land. Impressment continued. And the British refused to lift the blockade.

The problems got worse. Finally, the United States declared war on June 18, 1812. The fighting soon focused on two main areas. One was the land around the Great Lakes. The other was the Atlantic Ocean.

Major Events

As the War of 1812 progressed, neither side was able to achieve a key victory that would lead to the war ending in their favor. The **Treaty** of Ghent ended the conflict without a clear victor.

April 27, 1813

U.S. forces successfully capture and burn the city of York, now known as Toronto.

June 20, 1812

President James Madison signs a declaration of war on Great Britain.

January 22, 1813

American soldiers are killed after a battle at the River Raisin. The phrase "Remember the Raisin" is used by U.S. soldiers to remember the massacre.

When the U.S. Senate voted on whether to declare war on Great Britain, 19 senators voted in favor of the war, while 13, including Chauncey Goodrich, voted against it.

August 24–25, 1814

British forces attack Washington, D.C., and burn government buildings, including the Capitol and the White House.

December 24, 1814

The Treaty of Ghent is signed to end the war. It restores the relationship between the combatants to its pre-war state.

September 12–14, 1814

A British attempt to capture the city of Baltimore fails when soldiers are unable to take Fort McHenry.

During the War of 1812, many early battles focused on forts.

Chapter 2
The Great Lakes

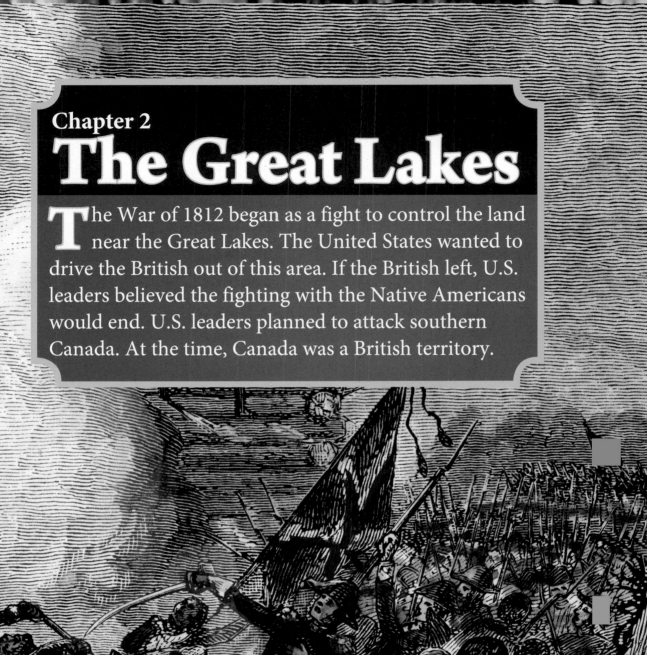

The War of 1812 began as a fight to control the land near the Great Lakes. The United States wanted to drive the British out of this area. If the British left, U.S. leaders believed the fighting with the Native Americans would end. U.S. leaders planned to attack southern Canada. At the time, Canada was a British territory.

Many U.S. leaders thought the British would **surrender** this territory without a fight. After all, the best British troops were busy fighting in France. In addition, only 500,000 people lived in Canada, not counting Native Americans. The United States had a population of 7.7 million and could put together a larger army.

William Hull was the governor of the Michigan Territory. He accepted a commission as a brigadier general when the war began.

U.S. troops marched toward Fort Detroit. They planned to attack nearby British forts in Canada. But they soon ran into problems. Woods and swamps slowed the soldiers. The British had time to rush new troops into place. In fact, the British took Fort Mackinac in July 1812. This U.S. fort was near Lake Huron.

In August 1812, William Hull led U.S. forces across the Detroit River into Canada. But the British and their Native American allies chased him back to U.S. soil. They followed him to Fort Detroit and pounded it with cannonballs. Hull surrendered. Everyone was shocked. The British now stood on U.S. territory.

Other U.S. losses piled up. A group of Native Americans from the Potawatomi group attacked Fort Dearborn and burned it. A U.S. attack on Montreal, Canada's most important city, went nowhere. An invasion of Canada from New York also failed. By January 1813, the British and their Native American allies had defeated U.S. forces west of Fort Detroit. They could now attack the U.S. settlers in Ohio.

In September 1813, Oliver Hazard Perry led U.S. ships from Ohio. He attacked British ships that were patrolling Lake Erie. The fleets fired at each other for hours. But Perry eventually won the battle.

Perry's victory cleared the way for the United States to drive the British from Fort Detroit later that month. The British and their Native American allies had to **retreat** into Canada. U.S. forces defeated them in October. The United States had taken control of the frontier.

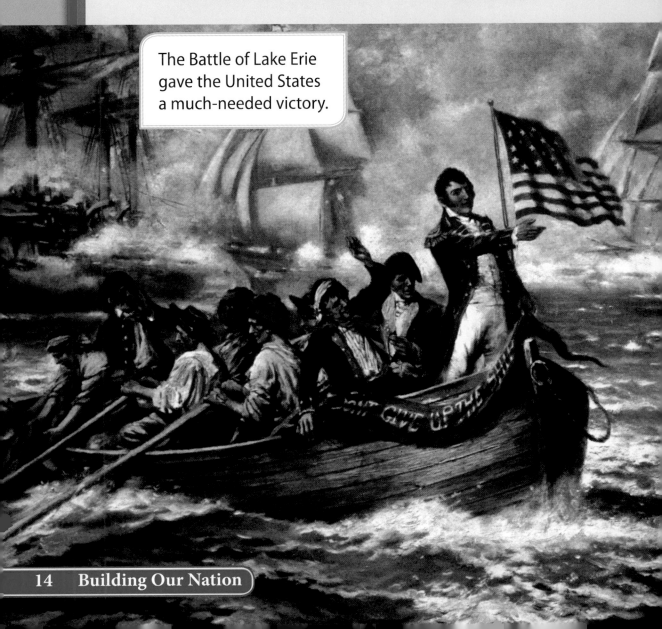

The Battle of Lake Erie gave the United States a much-needed victory.

Major Battles

During the War of 1812, both British and American forces achieved numerous victories and suffered several defeats. While the United States was not able to hold southern Canada, the nation was able to win key battles against the powerful British Royal Navy.

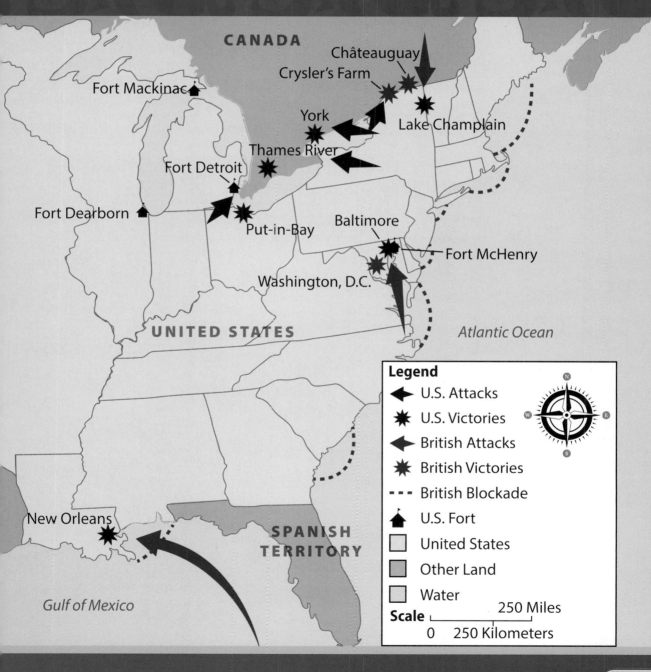

CANADA

Fort Mackinac

Châteauguay

Crysler's Farm

York

Lake Champlain

Thames River

Fort Detroit

Fort Dearborn

Put-in-Bay

Baltimore

Fort McHenry

Washington, D.C.

UNITED STATES

Atlantic Ocean

New Orleans

SPANISH TERRITORY

Gulf of Mexico

Legend
- ◀ U.S. Attacks
- ✸ U.S. Victories
- ◀ British Attacks
- ✸ British Victories
- - - - British Blockade
- 🔺 U.S. Fort
- ☐ United States
- ☐ Other Land
- ☐ Water

Scale

250 Miles

0   250 Kilometers

Tecumseh

Tecumseh was the leader of the Shawnees. At first, he said it was foolish for Native Americans and U.S. settlers to fight. He called people on both sides "little children who only scratch each other's faces." But as U.S. soldiers tried to take Native American land, Tecumseh worked to unite many groups. He called them to "rise as one man" and fight back. He dreamed of a separate Native American nation.

When the War of 1812 began, Tecumseh joined the British. He led all their Native American allies. The British agreed to create an independent Native American nation if they won. Tecumseh's forces helped the British capture Fort Detroit and invade Ohio. However, U.S. soldiers eventually forced them to retreat to Canada.

Tecumseh died in battle on October 5, 1813. After his death, the alliance between the Native Americans and the British fell apart. Tecumseh is still admired for his leadership and intelligence.

Chapter 3
Struggles at Sea

As soldiers clashed near the Great Lakes, other battles took place on the Atlantic Ocean. Here, the United States faced the powerful British Royal Navy. The U.S. Navy had only 16 ships. The British had 584. Even so, the U.S. Navy started strong. In August 1812, the USS *Constitution* defeated the HMS *Guerriere*. During the fight, a British shot bounced off the side of the *Constitution*. The ship was then nicknamed "Old Ironsides."

The USS *Constitution* survived the War of 1812. Today, it is the world's oldest commissioned naval ship still floating.

U.S. ships won two more battles that year. But the Royal Navy remained far stronger. In 1813, British ships blockaded the U.S. coast. They easily took control of the Chesapeake Bay. This bay connects Baltimore, Maryland, to the Atlantic Ocean. It also passes near Washington, D.C. The British were closing in on the U.S. capital.

U.S. Casualties During the War of 1812

During the War of 1812, the U.S. military suffered losses both on land and at sea. The majority of deaths were caused by sickness and disease, not by British weaponry.

Branch	Deaths	Non-Fatal Injuries
Army	1,950	4,000
Navy	265	439
Marines	45	66
Total	2,260	4,505

In Europe, the British defeated the French in the spring of 1814. New ships and soldiers came to the United States. In August, the British attacked Washington, D.C. They encountered U.S. forces at Bladensburg, Maryland. This city was less than 10 miles (16 km) from the capital. British troops smashed through the defense in three hours.

The British soldiers marched into Washington, D.C., the same afternoon. Soldiers burned most of the government buildings, including the White House. A fierce storm hit the city as it burned. The British were surprised by the weather and left quickly.

British soldiers set fire to government buildings in Washington, D.C., in response to the burning of York by Americans the previous year.

Next, the British aimed at Baltimore. This city had a **harbor** used by U.S. ships. Fort McHenry defended the harbor. On September 13, 1814, British ships fired cannonballs, rockets, and bombs at Fort McHenry. But they barely damaged the fort's strong walls. The fort survived the attack. Unable to do more, the Royal Navy sailed out of the Chesapeake Bay.

During the Battle of Baltimore, Fort McHenry was attacked by 16 British ships.

The war was reaching a standstill. Each side could damage the other. But neither could win. Leaders in the two countries grew tired of losing soldiers, ships, and money. They began discussing peace.

The end of the war focused on the city of New Orleans.

Chapter 4
Making Peace

Despite talks of peace, the war dragged on. The British blockade stretched all the way across the Gulf of Mexico. In 1814, the British planned to attack New Orleans, Louisiana. This city was an important U.S. port. Andrew Jackson took charge of defending it. But he needed more troops. He **drafted** locals to help. Many were volunteers. They had little experience fighting.

Far away, British and U.S. **diplomats** discussed peace. They signed a peace treaty in Ghent, Belgium, in December 1814. The Treaty of Ghent did not declare a winner. The two countries simply agreed to stop fighting.

It took two months for word of the treaty to reach the United States. In the meantime, fighting continued. On January 8, 1815, U.S. troops defeated the British at the Battle of New Orleans. Finally, the U.S. Congress approved the peace treaty on February 16, 1815. The War of 1812 was officially over.

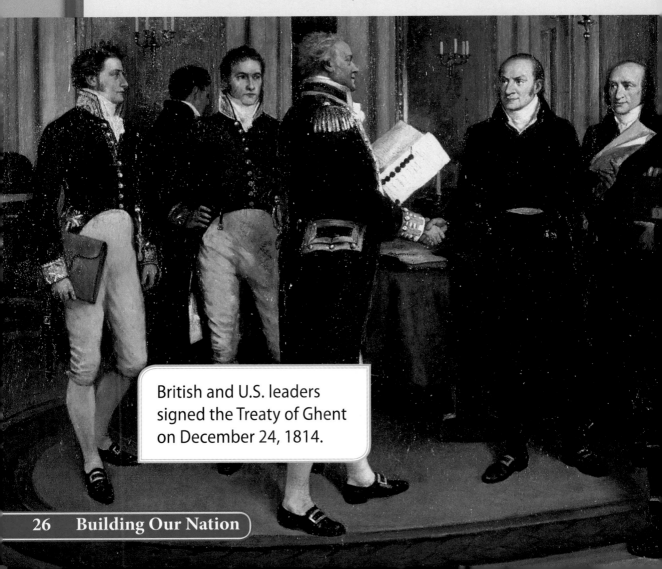

British and U.S. leaders signed the Treaty of Ghent on December 24, 1814.

Fighting the war had cost the United States lives and money. But the young country had stood its ground against the powerful British. The many U.S. states had fought together as a single nation.

After the war, British leaders treated the United States with more respect. Other European countries, such as France and Spain, also began to treat the United States as an equal.

The War of 1812 was a disaster for Native Americans. Fighting, diseases, and hunger killed

thousands of people. Many groups never recovered. After the war, settlers continued stealing their lands. To make matters worse, the British stopped helping their former allies. Many groups were forced to sign peace treaties that gave away their homelands. Settlers poured into these new areas.

Throughout the 1800s, settlers pushed west toward the Pacific Ocean. Many Native American nations resisted them in a long series of wars. Fighting did not end until 1890. By then, much of today's United States had taken shape.

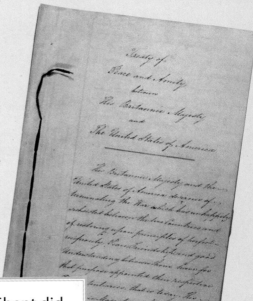

The final text of the Treaty of Ghent did not mention impressment. This left a major cause of the war unresolved.

A **10-year** period of political cooperation in the United States followed the War of 1812. It is known as the **"Era of Good Feelings."**

About **20,000** soldiers **died** during the **War of 1812**.

The **last veteran** of the War of 1812 **died** in **1905**.

U.S. Expansion after 1815

After the conclusion of the war, the United States continued to grow in size. This expansion included the purchasing of territories and the signing of new treaties to acquire land.

Oregon Country: Divided between Great Britain and the United States by the Oregon Treaty in 1846

Maine and New Brunswick Boundary: Established by the Webster–Ashburton Treaty with Britain in 1842

Red River Basin: Acquired from Britain in the Convention of 1818

Mexican Cession: Gained by the Treaty of Guadalupe Hidalgo in 1848

Atlantic Ocean

Texas Annexation: Became a state in 1845

Florida Cession: Gained by the Adams–Onís Treaty with Spain in 1819

Gadsden Purchase: Purchased from Mexico in 1853

Gulf of Mexico

Legend

- ■ Mexican Cession
- ☐ Gadsden Purchase
- ■ Oregon Country
- ■ Red River Basin
- ■ Maine and New Brunswick Boundary
- ■ Florida Cession
- ■ Texas Annexation
- ☐ United States (1815)
- ■ Other Land
- ☐ Water

Scale

250 Miles

0   250 Kilometers

Quiz

1 What document ended the war?

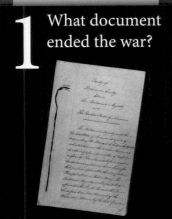

2 What was the population of the United States in 1812?

3 What nickname was given to the USS *Constitution*?

4 What city was attacked by American forces on April 27, 1813?

5 How many U.S. citizens were forced to serve in the Royal Navy between 1807 and 1812?

6 How many British ships attacked Fort McHenry?

7 Which side did Tecumseh support during the war?

8 How long did the War of 1812 last?

Answer: 1. The Treaty of Ghent **2.** 7.7 million **3.** "Old Ironsides" **4.** York **5.** More than 6,000 **6.** 16 **7.** The British **8.** 2 years and 8 months

Key Words

allies: nations or people that are on the same side during a war

blockade: when an area is closed off so nothing can go in or out

diplomats: people who represent their country's government

drafted: required someone to serve in the military

frontier: an area at the edge of a settled or developed territory or country

harbor: a calm body of water where ships can take shelter or tie up to the land

negotiate: to discuss ways to solve a problem

retreat: to move away from battle

surrender: to stop fighting and give up

treaty: an official agreement between groups

Index

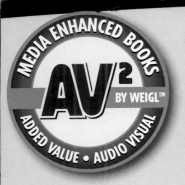

Log on to www.av2books.com

AV² by Weigl brings you media enhanced books that support active learning. Go to www.av2books.com, and enter the special code found on page 2 of this book. You will gain access to enriched and enhanced content that supplements and complements this book. Content includes video, audio, weblinks, quizzes, a slide show, and activities.

AV² Online Navigation

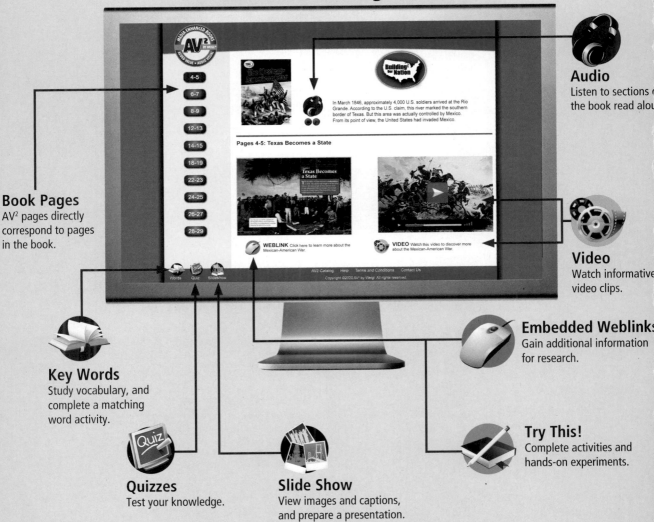

Audio
Listen to sections of the book read aloud

Book Pages
AV² pages directly correspond to pages in the book.

Video
Watch informative video clips.

Key Words
Study vocabulary, and complete a matching word activity.

Embedded Weblinks
Gain additional information for research.

Quizzes
Test your knowledge.

Slide Show
View images and captions, and prepare a presentation.

Try This!
Complete activities and hands-on experiments.

AV² was built to bridge the gap between print and digital. We encourage you to tell us what you like and what you want to see in the future.

Sign up to be an AV² Ambassador at www.av2books.com/ambassador.

Due to the dynamic nature of the Internet, some of the URLs and activities provided as part of AV² by Weigl may have changed or ceased to exist. AV² by Weigl accepts no responsibility for any such changes. All media enhanced books are regularly monitored to update addresses and sites in a timely manner. Contact AV² by Weigl at 1-866-649-3445 or av2books@weigl.com with any questions, comments, or feedback.